Praise for *Why Jews Do That*

"What Steph Curry is to the three-pointer, Avram Mlotek is to rabbi-ing. Let him —and this book—be your guide to a deeper understanding of Judaism."

Bari Weiss
Author of How to Fight Anti-Semitism *and staff editor and writer for* The New York Times

"If you want a 'Judaism for Dummies' with a shmear of snark and potty mouth, this is the book for you."

Jackie Hoffman
Emmy-nominated comedian and Fiddler On The Roof In Yiddish's Yenta, the Matchmaker

"Rabbi Avram Mlotek draws people into Jewish life with his enthusiasm, his warmth, his music, and his understanding that people are often embarrassed to ask even the most basic questions. Here, he makes those questions fun and accessible to all."

Eric Fingerhut
President, Jewish Federations of North America and past President of Hillel International

"Learning basic information about Judaism is often ponderous and, as a result, many people never learn it. But in the capable, consistently accurate and sometimes irreverent hands of Avram Mlotek, the process becomes both fun and funny."

Rabbi Joseph Telushkin
Author of The New York Times *bestseller* Rebbe *and* Jewish Literacy

"Finally! A book about Jews written entirely in questions! Is that perfect? Reb Mlotek, adank for this bukh! (Thanks for this book!)"

Julie Klausner
Creator and star of Hulu's Difficult People

"As someone who has undergone a conversion journey to Judaism with Rabbi Avram, I can truly say that he is not an ordinary rabbi. And neither is this book. I highly recommend it to people who are seeking to learn Jewish fundamentals but in a modern, hip, and entertaining way."

Ruta Gyvyte
Lithuanian model and Instagram influencer

Skyhorse Publishing

WHY JEWS DO THAT

OR 30 QUESTIONS YOUR RABBI NEVER ANSWERED

Jewgle

🔍 why do jews

🔍 why do jews celebrate passover

🔍 why do jews celebrate hanukkah

🔍 why do jews eat kosher

🔍 why do jews eat brisket

🔍 why do jews wear suits

🔍 why do jews write g-d

Jewgle Search   I'm Feeling Kosher

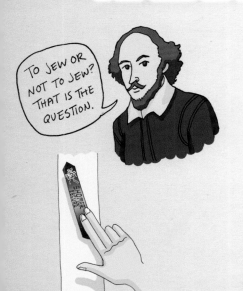

To Jew or not to Jew? That is the question.

SHOMER SHABBOS!

AVRAM MLOTEK

ILLUSTRATIONS BY FABY RODRIGUEZ AND JENNY YOUNG

MITZVAH TANK

For Revaya, Hillel Yosl, and Shabtai: keep the questions coming.

Skyhorse Publishing books may be purchased in bulk at special discounts for sales promotion, corporate gifts, fund-raising, or educational purposes. Special editions can also be created to specifications. For details, contact the Special Sales Department, Skyhorse Publishing, 307 West 36th Street, 11th Floor, New York, NY 10018 or info@skyhorsepublishing.com.

Skyhorse® and Skyhorse Publishing® are registered trademarks of Skyhorse Publishing, Inc.®, a Delaware corporation.

Visit our website at www.skyhorsepublishing.com.

10 9 8 7 6 5 4 3 2 1

Library of Congress Cataloging-in-Publication Data is available on file.

Cover design by Brian Peterson

Print ISBN: 978-1-5107-6049-3
Ebook ISBN: 978-1-5107-6050-9

Printed in China

Table of Questions

Introduction

Merry Hanukkah! Happy Passover! Tired of Googling every time your grandmother refers to some obscure Jewish holiday? Wish you had an easy-to-read and hilarious bathroom-like book that you aren't afraid of leaving in the bathroom when your grandmother actually comes over to visit? Fear no more and welcome to *Why Jews Do That? Or 30 Questions Your Rabbi Never Answered.*

Like the Bible, this book has five fundamental sections: Time, Props, Purpose, Grub, and God. Unlike the Author of that canonical text, this author is a millennial who serves as a rabbi for millennials. Each question in this book is accompanied by a response, a fun fact (often tangentially related), as well as a "Jew, say wha?" quote where famous Jewish ideas and wizards are referenced. Cartoons and illustrations have been created by dear students of mine from Base, Jenny Young and Faby Rodriguez.

Judaism is a way of life full of questions and inquiry. From the Biblical Abraham questioning God's righteousness to The Four Questions of Passover night, questions have always been a fundamental feature of Judaism. Why? Why not? To ask is to wonder, to question is to open ourselves to the ongoing learning of life. Answers are way less important, so maybe don't even read further. No, explanations are definitely needed; just be wary of the autocratic dogmatist rabbi in your midst.

Bottom line: this book is for you, whoever Jew are. Ask away.

RAM

TIME

Faby Rodriguez

"I'm Shomer Frigen Shabbos" Means What Exactly?

We've all seen *The Big Lebowski*, the cult classic Coen brothers film where John Goodman's character shouts, "I'm shomer frigen *Shabbos*!" But besides refusing to frequent bowling alleys, what does "shomer frigen Shabbos" actually mean? Shabbos, or Shabbat, refers to the Jewish day of rest, the Sabbath, which occurs every week. From sundown on Friday afternoon till Saturday night when three stars emerge, Shabbos is considered a weekly holiday in the Jewish calendar. "Shomer" is Hebrew for guardian or keeper. Hence, shomer Shabbos: a Sabbath keeper.

So, what's a keeper? Note the first question by humankind in the Torah (Cain to God: "Am I my brother's keeper?") inferring some type of responsibility or rule following.[1] Speaking of rules, the Ten Commandments appear twice in the Torah: once in Exodus where the command is to "remember" the Sabbath, and once in Deuteronomy where the instruction is to "keep" the Sabbath. The sixteenth-century Kabbalist poet Shlomo HaLevi Alkabetz wrote, "Remember and keep in one utterance," referring to how God can drop a beat and spit lyric at the same time. His liturgical poem is now recited in practically every Jewish house of worship on Friday nights.

JEW, SAY WHA?

> "Caesar asked Rabbi Joshua ben Chananya:
> 'Why do Shabbat foods smell so good?'
> Said he to him: 'We have a special spice,
> "Shabbat" is its name.'"
>
> *Babylonian Talmud, Shabbat 119a*

Keeping and remembering can mean vastly different things, though. Keeping usually refers to honoring the thirty-nine[2] forbidden creative labors prohibited on the Sabbath. Remembering? For some this means going to synagogue; for others it includes lighting candles (more on that later). Whether it's gathering for a home-cooked meal over a glass of wine[3] or refusing to go bowling, Shabbat is a differentiated and sacred time in the Jewish psyche.

SHOMER SHABBOS!

@JennyYoungArt

FUN FACT!
Long before WiFi and hotspots, the Sabbath served as the ultimate energizing rejuvenator and to this day strict observers will refuse to use electronics for the Sabbath's duration of twenty-five hours.

Faby Rodriguez

What's with Jews and Candles? Or Why Do I See Candelabras in the Windowsills in Winter?

Have you ever tried to eat in the dark? It's dreadful. Add some light, and that experience[4] becomes intimate, maybe joyous, perhaps even romantic. The Medieval Jewish commentator Maimonides declared that lighting candles before the Sabbath was about making it an enjoyable experience, seeing as starting a fire during the holy time is Biblically prohibited. Later, the *Code of Jewish Law* by Rabbi Yosef Karo ruled that one should light candles before the Sabbath or a holiday for "family harmony."[5] Again, to avoid bumping into stuff in the middle of the night. Today, even with electricity to the rescue, Jews light candles as a way of marking holy time. So, in addition to lighting candles before certain holidays, Jews might light a *yortseit* (Yiddish for year-time) candle to observe the anniversary of someone's death.

As for the winter lights? No, these are not indoor Jewish Christmas decorations. These are lights lit in honor of the holiday of Hanukkah, which celebrates the Maccabean victory over the Greco-Syrians in 165 BCE, the discovery of a tiny jug of oil with supernatural qualities, and the subsequent rededication of the Ancient Temple.

JEW, SAY WHA?

> "These lights we kindle, in honor of the miracles and wonders, the salvation wrought and wars You fought, for our elders, in olden days and now . . . these lights are holy. "
>
> *Traditional Hanukkah Liturgy*

@JennyYoungArt

Since extinguishing flames are prohibited on Shabbat, traditional Jews leave candles lit till they burn out (same goes for Hanukkah candles). Public Service Announcement: One should never leave kindled lights unattended under any circumstances. Saving human life trumps all commandments.[6,7]

FUN FACT!

The Torah states that a human being is like God's candle[8] and in synagogues there is a *ner tamid*, eternal flame, which hangs over the ark where the Torah scroll is kept.

Faby Rodriguez

Is There a Jewish Halloween?

No, but Jews have a day even more raucous. A day where any person in need must be given charity,[9] a day where even the strictest of Orthodox rabbis say cross-dressing is permitted,[10] a day where Jewish law mandates one become so intoxicated that they do not know the difference between the protagonist and antagonist of a certain Biblical tale.[11] The holiday is Purim, and the tale is the Scroll of Esther, found in your local Bible.

JEW, SAY WHA?

> **"**From sorrow to gladness, from mourning to good days, they should make them days of feasting and merriment, and of sending gifts to another, and gifts to the poor. **»**
>
> *The Scroll of Esther, 9:2-2*

Purim tells the story of a Jewish Persian heroine, Esther, who saved her people from a sinister minister, Haman, who had a thing against the Jews (a storyline throughout our peoples' history). Esther won the empire-wide beauty contest conducted by King Ahasuerus. God is nowhere to be explicitly mentioned or named in this Biblical book, leading mystical commentators to discover the ancient game of "hide and seek," or, as it's known in rabbinic jargon, *hester panim*. When God is nowhere to be found, how might *you* act?

The story is full of topsy-turvy turns, and as a way of celebrating, Jews will read the scroll, give gifts to one another and to the less fortunate, and dress up in drag. Purim: also known as the Jewish Mardi Gras.

@JennyYoungArt

FUN FACT!

Long before the 45th President of the United States would send tweets in the middle of night, King Ahasuerus (who also held beauty contests) would read from the *Book of Records* when he couldn't sleep.

Do Jews Fast?

We all know Jews love to eat but do they fast, too? Yep, big time. There are all different types of fasts in Judaism: fasts where folks cease speaking and fasts where folks cease eating. In Judaism, when we fast, this includes abstaining from both eating and drinking . . . and that even includes water![12] There are the Biblically mandated ones; that's Yom Kippur (the Jewish Day of Atonement), and then there are the fasts decreed by the rabbis of the Talmud. They include the following: the 9th of Av (*Tisha b'Av*), where Jews mourn the destruction of the First and Second Temples and other calamitous occasions (boy, do we have a few!); the 17th of Tammuz, which commemorates the breaching of the walls of Jerusalem in the First Temple period; and the 10th of Tevet, in memory of the siege of Jerusalem by the King of Babylon, Nebuchadnezzar (say that five times fast!). There's also the third of *Tishrei*, known as *Tzom Gedaliyah*, in memory of the slaying of Gedaliah, the first Jewish government official to be killed by fellow Jews. And there's Esther's Fast, which lasts from dawn till dusk on Purim eve; it commemorates the three-day fast the Jews held in the time of Queen Esther. Fasting is generally understood to be a certain type of body/heart/soul affliction (think *Eat, Pray, Love* sans "Eat").

Jew, say wha?

> **"**Why, when we fasted, did You not see? When we starved our bodies, did You pay no heed? Because on your fast day you see to your business and oppress all your laborers! Is such the fast I desire, a day for men to starve their bodies? Do you call that a fast, a day when the Lord is favorable? No, this is the fast I desire: To unlock fetters of wickedness, and untie the cords of the yoke, to let the oppressed go free, to break off every yoke. It is to share your bread with the hungry, and to take the wretched poor into your home; when you see the naked, to clothe him, and not to ignore your own kin.**"**
>
> *Isaiah 58*

@JennyYoungArt

FUN FACT!

Jewish law believes that an especially pious person should fast every single Monday and Thursday, in remembrance of past Jewish tragedies.[13]

Why Does My Jewish Coworker Have a Million Holidays?

As Rabbi Adam Sandler once put it, "Instead of one night of presents, we get eight crazy nights." To be fair, the rabbis of the Talmud didn't exactly intend Hanukkah to compete with the Christmas shopping season. (If anything, the practice around giving and receiving Hanukkah *gelt*/money came from the practice of giving gifts to those less fortunate.)[14] And while Jews don't have a million holidays, per se, there are quite a few. There are the big dogs: Rosh Hashanah (the Jewish new year), Yom Kippur (the Day of Atonement), Hanukkah (Festival of Lights), and Passover (Freedom Festival). But there are others of equal importance, like Shavuot (celebrating the receiving of the Torah) and Sukkot (The Booths Festival), Shemini Atzeret (The Eighth day of Gathering) and Simchat Torah (Joy of the Torah). There's Tu Bishvat (Tree day) and Lag b'Omer (33rd of the Omer). And, of course, Purim. And we even have some modern days as well: Yom Ha'atzmaut (Israel Independence Day) and Yom HaShoah (Holocaust Remembrance Day).

JEW, SAY WHA?

" On all other festivals and holy days, one should rejoice himself and give joy to the poor. If he rejoices alone without providing for the poor, his punishment is severe, since he rejoices alone without giving joy to another. Of him is written, 'I will spread dung upon your faces, the dung of your festivals.' (Malachi 2:3) "

Zohar 2:88b

Faby Rodriguez

FUN FACT!

The most commonly celebrated holiday by American Jews is Passover.[15] Even President Obama celebrated this redemptive holiday while in the White House.

Faby Rodriguez

Do Jews Believe in Heaven and Hell?

The short answer is yes and no, but not in the ways that you think. Confusing enough? There is such a thing as paradise, in Hebrew known as *gan eden*, the Garden of Eden, a.k.a. Adam and Eve's zip code (though they were later evicted). *Shamayim* is the other Hebrew term, for skies or heavens. There is a valley south of Jerusalem, once used for pagan child sacrifice (definitely not a *Jewish thing*), that is known as *Gei Hinnom* and is sometimes likened to a Jewish hell. There's *Olam Haba*, the world to come.[16] Finally, there's *Sheol*, which is some type of bottomless pit and where some believe all descend to for a brief period of time. Jewish liturgy describes a *Book of Life* that is referenced in high holiday prayer books but, depending who you ask, they'll tell you it's like Santa listing naughty/nice, or entirely metaphoric.

Jew, say wha?

"I am sated with misfortune; I am at the brink of Sheol. I am numbered with those who go down to the Pit; I am a helpless man abandoned among the dead, like bodies lying in the grave of whom You are mindful no more, and who are cut off from Your care. You have put me at the bottom of the Pit, in the darkest places, in the depths. **"**

Psalm 88:4-7

@JennyYoungArt

FUN FACT!

Jews tend to focus more on life than death. That's not to say we don't have plenty of thoughts about death and mourning, but our emphasis is very much on living. The drinking creed? *L'chayim!* To Life. This isn't just a *Fiddler On The Roof* quote; it's a framework for how to live according to the Torah.[17]

PROPS

Why Do Jews Wear Pope-Like Caps?

No, Moses did not wear a yarmulke. The source of covering one's head comes from the Babylonian Talmud in tractate Kiddushin, where the rabbis teach wearing a head covering; for short, it is a virtue of piety, expressing that the Divine dwells above.[18] *Yarmulke* in Yiddish (*Kippah* in Hebrew) is a small cloth cap worn by Jews. Some wear it only when praying, some when eating, and others wear it the whole day, making sure not to walk even a step without it.

In Israel, the type of kippah you wear can be a strong indicator for what type of political views you hold.[19] Large black typically equals Ultra Orthodox, whereas a knitted kippah often reflects adherence to religious Zionism (folks who believe Jews are religiously linked to the land). The same holds true for outside the State of Israel. If you see a man dressed in dark pants, a white shirt, and donning a velvet black yarmulke, chances are extremely high that the dude identifies as Orthodox.

Jew, Say Wha?

> "Because of our traditions we have kept our balance for many, many years. Here in Anatevka, we have traditions for everything: how to eat, how to sleep, how to wear clothes. For instance, we always keep our heads covered, and always wear a little prayer-shawl. This shows our constant devotion to God. You may ask, how did this tradition start? I'll tell you. I don't know. But it's a tradition. And because of our traditions, every one of us knows who he is and what God expects him to do."
>
> "Tevye," *Fiddler on the Roof*

@JennyYoungArt

FUN FACT!

In Orthodox communities, all men and boys wear yarmulkes. In egalitarian communities, women wear yarmulkes. Back in the day, Reform synagogues prohibited the wearing of yarmulkes in synagogue. The author of this book often wears a rainbow pride kippah.

Faby Rodriguez

What's with Hasidic Jew Garb?

If you've ever been to Boro Park or Williamsburg (not the hipster sections) in Brooklyn, New York, or certain religious communities in Israel, you've probably seen the Hasidic fashion style and might have even noticed slight differences in sock length and hats. In the Ultra-Orthodox community, different styles of socks and hats can denote different religious sects. On a spiritual level, wearing layers upon layers of dark clothing in the summer isn't meant to be masochistic, it's meant to be modest, or in Yiddish/Hebrew, *tznius*. Most married women in these religious communities cover their hair or wear wigs known as a *sheytl*, or *tichel*, a headscarf. Clothing is just one avenue of actualizing modesty values, motivating wearers toward increased mindfulness. Modesty, though, can also refer to speech and behavior.

JEW, SAY WHA?

> "Do justice, love kindness, walk modestly with your God."
>
> *Micah 6:8*

Hasidism was a movement of revival and spirituality born in the Ukraine in the eighteenth century. The root word of Hasidism stems from the Hebrew word, *hesed*, which means loving-kindness. Hasidism reintroduced the spiritual motifs and often esoteric values of Kabbalah—the foremost text on Jewish mysticism—back to the masses. Through song, story, dance, meditation, ecstatic prayer, friendship, and study, Hasidism replaced devotion to God at the center of Jewish life, along with the role of a *rebbe*, the spiritual head of a particular sect or community. How one of the most theologically and religiously groundbreaking movements became synonymous with some of the most conservative voices of Judaism today is worthy of further exploration. Look past the socks and wigs, folks.

@JennyYoungArt

FUN FACT!

Hasidic clothing was deeply influenced by the style of what Polish-Lithuanian secular nobility looked like in the eighteenth century.[20]

What's Inside the Funky Amulet Hanging on the Door?

So, you've just moved into a new apartment and your Jewish grandma gives you a bizarre amulet to hang on your door. No, she does not believe in witchcraft (well . . . she might, but not in this instance). A *mezuzah* literally means doorpost, and it's one of the oldest traditions around. The Torah instructs Jews to inscribe a certain section of the Bible[21] on "doorposts and on our gates, to bound upon our arms and between our eyes." A mezuzah contains a scroll inside, a *klaf*. It also contains one of the Hebrew names for the Divine, שדי in Hebrew, *ShaDaY*, which is an acronym for "Shomer Daltot Yisrael," or "Guardian of the Doors of Israel." Superstitiously inclined Jews often believe calamity or illness can be linked to a faulty klaf. Traditional Jews will kiss their hand after touching a mezuzah when entering or exiting a room (coronavirus notwithstanding. Seriously, rabbis have now counseled against this practice given the recent outbreak of the latest fatal plague).

JEW, SAY WHA?

> **"**The Lord will guard your goings and your comings, from now and forever. **"**
>
> *Psalm 121:8*

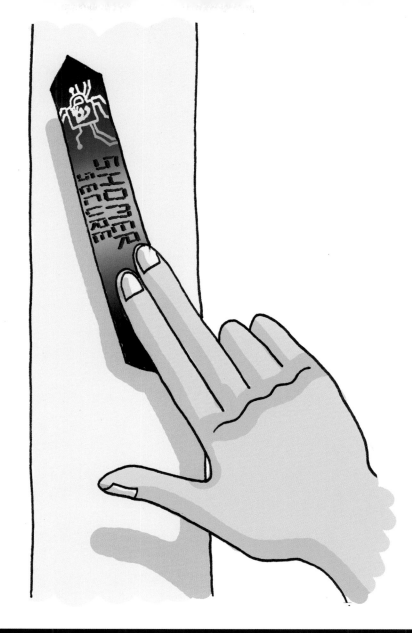

@JennyYoungArt

FUN FACT!

Synagogues do not technically require a mezuzah, as folks don't usually sleep there.
Neither do bathrooms.

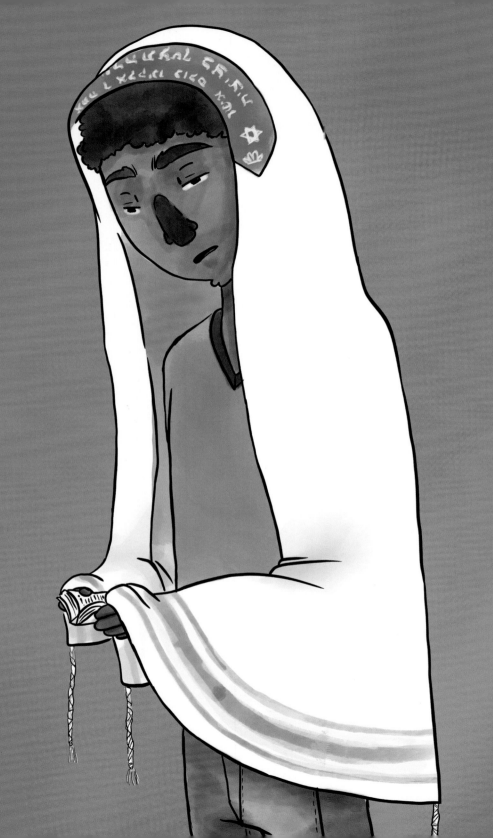

Faby Rodriguez

Why the Shawls in Shul?

If you walk into a synagogue, you may see folks donning a scarf-like shawl around their necks or larger blanket-like shawls which drape over their backs. This is the equivalent of the Jewish superhero cape, also known as a *tallit*. The Torah in Deuteronomy Chapter 22 commands, "You shall make yourself twisted cords, on the four corners of your garment with which you cover yourself." Those cords or strings are known as *tzitzit*, or tassels. Those tassels are then attached to the tallit which you see in synagogues. Some Jews wear a *tallit katan*, which is commonly known as tzitzit, under their shirts. According to the Bible,[22] the tzizit serve as a reminder of all the commandments and combine dress and apparel to God-like awareness. For those Jews who do choose to wear them outside their clothing, they must be tucked in when at a cemetery.[23] Some tzitzit have a blue turquoise-colored string known as the *techelet*, which according to the Talmud comes from a sea creature.

JEW, SAY WHA?

“Once there was a man, who was very careful about the commandment of tzitzit. He heard about a certain harlot in one of the towns by the sea who charged a fee of four hundred gold coins for her hire. He sent her four hundred gold coins in advance and scheduled a time to meet her. When his time arrived he came and sat at her doorstep. The harlot's maid told her: 'The man who sent you four hundred gold coins is here and is waiting at the door'; to which the harlot replied 'Let him come in.' He came in . . . She then went up to the top bed and sat upon it naked. He too went up and sat naked next to her, when suddenly the tzitzit of his garment struck him across the face; he slipped off the bed and fell upon the ground.”

Babylonian Talmud, Menachot 44a

@JennyYoungArt

FUN FACT!

While tzitzit are generally worn by men (even in the scorching summer), there is a growing number of women and gender-fluid folks who are taking this commandment upon themselves.

ברוך אתה יי, אלהינו מלך העולם,

בורא פרי הגפן

ברוך אתה יי, אלהינו מלך העולם,

אשר בחר בנו מכל-עם, ורוממנו מכל-לשון,

וקדשנו במצותיו.

ותתן-לנו י

מועדים לש   שון

את-יום חג   רותנו,

מקרא קדש   ים.

כי בנו בחרת   ל-העמים.

ומועדי קד   הנחלתנו.

ברוך אתה   זמנים

ברוך אתה יי א   העולם,

שהחינו וקימנו וה   לזמן הזה

What's with the KKK? Kiddush, Kaddish, and Kadosh?

In Hebrew, all words have a *shoresh*, or root word. In this way, all of the Hebrew language can be poetically interlaced. These three words share the same *shoresh*, or root word: קדש. *Kadosh* means holy or sacred. *Kiddush* is the blessing and sanctification made over wine. (Nearly all Jewish celebrations involve making a *L'chayim* (toast to life) over grape juice or wine.) Kiddush most typically refers to the blessing over wine made on Shabbat or on the holidays. *Kaddish* is the memorial prayer recited by mourners after a loved one has passed away.

JEW, SAY WHA?

> **"**What came is gone forever every time.**"**
>
> *Allen Ginsburg's Kaddish*

The KKK is a racist, xenophobic, and anti-semitic hate group that has no relation to the three Hebrew terms that begin with K; to that end, you can be sure the author's grandmother is not particularly pleased with the snarky title of this question.

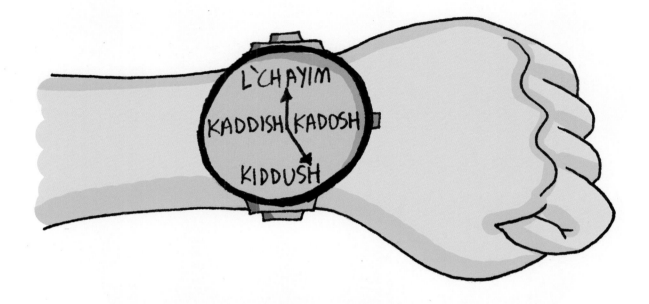

@JennyYoungArt

FUN FACT!

Jewish law prohibits all snacking and drinking before kiddush once the time to fulfill this commandment has arrived.[24] Seriously, can you imagine Jews without snacks?

Is Mikvah a Jewish Spa?

Wax on, wax off. That's the general idea. Enter impure, emerge cleansed. A *mikvah* is a Jewish ritual bath, which must be connected to a stream, spring—essentially, rain water. Jewish law requires anyone who converts to Judaism to immerse, as well as after a woman's menstrual cycle prior to resuming sexual relations. (Yep, Jewish law goes there.) Some Hasidic men go to the mikvah before every Sabbath, and some even go every morning. Women and men tend to go before getting married.

There's a growing practice for grooms to immerse before their weddings, and gender non-conforming folks utilize the mikvah with current trends in place to modernize these ancient customs. Some communities even have a *kelim* mikvah, a mikvah specifically used for immersing dishes in order to make them kosher.[25]

JEW, SAY WHA?

> "The ritual bath of Israel is the Lord."
>
> *Jeremiah 17*

Traditionally, a mikvah is the first structure built when establishing a Jewish community, even before a synagogue or school. One enters the mikvah in their birthday suit; nail polish, jewelry, hair clips, and piercings must all be removed so that water can enter every pore of the body.

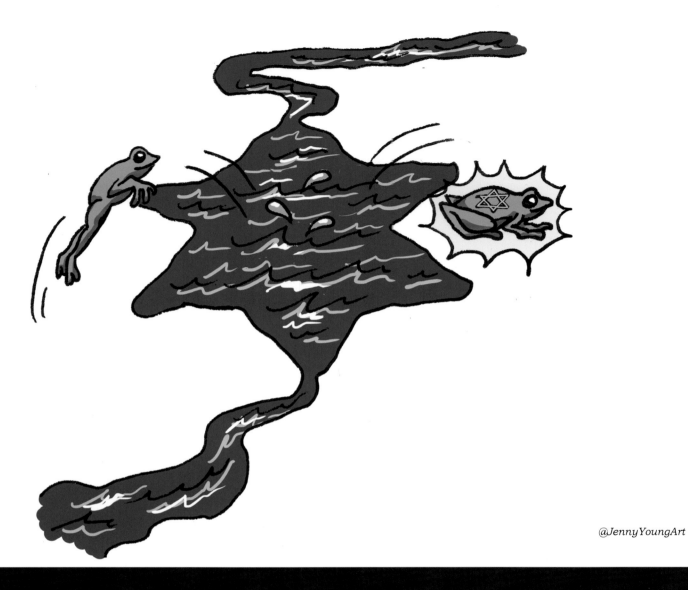

@JennyYoungArt

FUN FACT!

Mikvah has typically been shrouded in secrecy, but mikvah life did make national headlines recently when a prominent Washington, DC rabbi was arrested, convicted, and imprisoned for voyeurism, where he recorded videos of women going to the mikvah. This raised dialogue within the American Orthodox community around male power in a female space. Generally, a convert is required to immerse before a *Beit Din*, a ritual court of three rabbis. Practices vary as to whether or not the Beit Din need be present at the time of immersion or whether or not a Mikvah guide can suffice.

PURPOSE

Faby Rodriguez

Reform, Conservative, Orthodox: Which Are the Jews Who Have Horns?

A Jew is stuck on an island. When he finally gets rescued, he shows his rescuers where he has lived. "This was my house," he says. "This was my synagogue." The rescuers notice another synagogue-type building and ask, "Why the second one?" To which the Jew replies, "That's the synagogue I don't go to." Do you know the adage, "One Jew, two opinions"? Well, Judaism has always had its tribes (See Jacob's sons: i.e., twelve tribes). But today, there are basically three major different denominations within Judaism: Orthodox, Conservative, and Reform. There's also Renewal and Reconstructionist. What marks their differences, among other things, is their relationship to *halacha*, Jewish law, and the extent to which the movements understand Jewish law to be binding.

JEW, SAY WHA?

> **"**In order to be a really successful leader you have to be just a little bit ahead of your community, and make sure that you're bringing them along; but if you're too far ahead of your community, you're just seen as a kook. **"**
>
> *Rabba Sara Hurwitz, pioneering Orthodox female rabbi,*
>
> *quoting Rabbi Yitz Greenberg*

Today, most young Jews don't go to synagogue or affiliate denominationally, so there are new emerging titles of "Just Jewish," or "Post-denominational," or "nondenominational." The differences are both important and unimportant. Important insomuch as it allows folks to have a clear sense of who they are, and unimportant in that it undermines the common fabric we Jews all supposedly share.

Jews having horns is an anti-semitic trope that originated around medieval times. In Exodus 34:35, the Torah describes how light beams emanated from Moses. How light became horns is thanks to the poetic misreading of Hebrew.

FUN FACT!

While synagogues may have different *siddurim* (Hebrew for prayer books), the liturgy would be the same in any traditional Conservative, Orthodox, or even Ultra-Orthodox synagogue, meaning Jews from all over the world from a plethora of divergent backgrounds might very well be saying the same thing every Saturday morning.

Faby Rodriguez

Why Do I Get Asked to Put on Black Boxes by Some Jews in the Middle of Times Square?

Jews don't missionize. But there is a term called *kiruv*, which means closeness. This is part of a mission by some religious groups to bring Jews closer to Judaism. Chabad is one of many ultra-Orthodox sects in the world but the singular most welcoming of other Jews. Founded by Rabbi Schneur Zalman of Liadi in the 1700s, Chabad is a Hebrew acronym for the first Hebrew letters of the following three words: *Chachma*, *Bina*, and *Daas*. Wisdom, understanding, and knowledge.

Rabbi Menachem Mendl Schneerson, the Lubavitcher Rebbe (or leader of Chabad), sent rabbinic couples all over the world to build Chabad Houses where kosher food would be readily available. As the saying goes, "Where there's a Coke, there's a Chabad." If you've ever been in New York, you may have encountered Chabad emissaries asking folks as they leave the subway if they're Jewish. And if the answer is yes, they'll give women candles to light for Shabbat and invite men to put on tefillin or phylacteries. If it's Sukkot, they'll invite Jews to shake the *lulav* (palm branch) and *etrog* (citrus), and if it's Hanukkah, they have public Hanukkah lightings in addition to giving out free candles and candelabras.

Jew, say wha?

> 66Intolerance lies at the core of evil. Not the intolerance that results from any threat or danger. But intolerance of another being who dares to exist. Intolerance without cause. It is so deep within us, because every human being secretly desires the entire universe to himself. Our only way out is to learn compassion without cause. To care for each other simply because that 'other' exists. 99
>
> *Rabbi Menachem Mendel Schneerson, the 7th Lubavitcher Rebbe*

While some experience Chabad as proselytizing, they rarely seek to convert non-Jews and their impact on Jewish life in America is undeniable. There is debate as to how much of Chabad believes Rabbi Schneerson was the Messiah; in many Chabad communities you can see signs in Hebrew, which read, "Long live the King Messiah!" with a picture of the Rebbe's face.

FUN FACT!

The Chabad Telethon has featured such celebrities as Bob Dylan, Magic Johnson, Adam Sandler, Kareem Abdul-Jabbar, and Whoopi Goldberg, among others.

What's with Israel and Why Do People Get So Upset Talking about It?

Israel is a country, a Biblical patriarch, a people, and an idea that has been around—in one way or another—for thousands of years. While the modern State of Israel is but seventy years young, Jews have lived in Israel since the times of the Bible. The Bible describes Israel as a "stiff-necked and stubborn"[26] people, and that wasn't even describing us when food is involved.

Judaism views the land of Israel as the permanent rental property of the Jewish people, meaning it's theirs so long as they don't mess up their divine covenant with the Creator.[27]

JEW, SAY WHA?

> "Living in the land of Israel is equivalent to performing all the commandments of the Torah."
>
> *Sifrei Deuteronomy 28*

Israel is the artist formerly known as Jacob (ever since his name change), and in Hebrew means "God wrestler."[28] For most of Jewish history, Jews have lived in the diaspora (meaning outside the land of Israel), but the return to Zion was always prominent in Jewish liturgy, with Jerusalem and Israel mentioned more times than you can count in daily prayers. There were many phases of immigration to Israel throughout history, but most notably would happen to be since the establishment of the modern State of Israel in 1948. As of today, Israel contains the majority of the world's Jewish population. As to why people get so upset: 1) go read about the Israeli/Arab conflict, and 2) Israel has become the "Jew" of the nations and Jews have always served as a convenient scapegoat.

Just as religious Zionists recite celebratory Psalms with a blessing using God's name to mark the establishment of the secular state, so too do some progressive Orthodox thinkers believe celebratory Psalms with a blessing using God's name ought to be recited when Israel and Palestine sign a peace treaty.

@JennyYoungArt

FUN FACT!

The term Jews use for moving to Israel is called making *aliyah*, which means ascent or going up. (Jerusalem is also about 2,700 feet above sea level.) This is also the same term used when being called to the Torah to recite a blessing.

Mo' Money, Mo' Problems: What's the Jewish Word for Charity?

Jews believe in charity but that is not what we call *tzedaka*. Tzedaka is derived from the Hebrew word *tzedek*, which means righteousness or justice.[29] *Nedava* is a donation or charity. Tzedaka, or giving tzedaka, is righteous and it is a mandated part of Jewish life, according to Jewish law. Jews are expected to give 10 percent of their income to tzedaka. Maimonides wrote at length what the highest form of tzedaka was "strengthening their hand until they are no longer dependent upon others." The sages teach, though, that when a person is unable to give any money or food, one must still address the person asking. Some rabbis of the Talmud would even give charity to those in need before they started their morning prayers, emphasizing that Jewish spirituality is inherently tied in with service of others and not just of self.

JEW, SAY WHA?

> **"**Give to the poor without knowing to whom one gives, and without the recipient knowing from who he received. For this is performing a mitzvah solely for the sake of Heaven.**"**
>
> *Maimonides, Mishne Torah, Laws on Charity*

THE HIGHEST FORM OF CHARITY:

@JennyYoungArt

FUN FACT!

There are special *pushkes* (Yiddish for charity box) in synagogues that are distributed at certain times throughout the weekday prayers and kept in Jewish homes. No charity is collected on the Sabbath, since handling money is forbidden.

I've Heard of the Torah; WTF Is the Talmud?

Jews don't call the Old Testament the Old Testament. Old implies there's something new, which is why Christians refer to the text in that way. Jews will, instead, call the text the Five Books of Moses, the Bible, the Torah, and the *TaNaKh* (which is an acronym in Hebrew for Torah, Prophets/Nvi'im and Writings/Ketuvim). That's all scripture. But Jews didn't stop writing after they left the promised land. The Talmud is a collection of the writings of the rabbis, the Mishna (codified in the second century) and the Gemara. The Mishna has six orders: Seeds, Festival, Women, Damages, Holies, and Purities, and each of these orders have multiple tractates.

JEW, SAY WHA?

> **"**Rabbi Eliezer then said to them: If the law is in accordance with my opinion, Heaven will prove it. A Divine Voice emerged from Heaven and said: Why are you differing with Rabbi Eliezer, as the law is in accordance with his opinion in every place that he expresses an opinion? Rabbi Yehoshua stood on his feet and said: It is written: "It is not in heaven's hands." (Deuteronomy 30:12) . . . Rabbi Natan encountered Elijah the prophet and said to him: What did the Holy One, Blessed be He, do at that time, when Rabbi Yehoshua issued his declaration? Elijah: The Holy One, Blessed be He, smiled and said: My children have triumphed over Me; My children have triumphed over Me.**"**
>
> *Babylonian Talmud Bava Metzia 59b*

The Gemara includes centuries' worth of rabbinic exegesis on Mishnaic and Biblical texts. It delves into rabbinic law, debate, cooking recipes, stories, teachings, and more. Talmud literally means study. Mishna literally means repeated. Gemara literally means learning. There's the Talmud written in the Land of Israel and the Talmud from Babylon. Much of it serves as a basis for Jewish law and practice today.

A JEWISH CALENDAR.

FUN FACT!

If you learn a *daf yomi*, a daily page of Talmud, it will take you seven-and-a-half years to complete reading the entire cycle. Tens of thousands of Jews study this text daily, and over three hundred thousand Orthodox men gather for the *siyum hashas*, the completion ceremony of the cycle. In January 2020, thousands of women gathered for the first time ever in Jerusalem after completing the several year study cycle.

Do Jews Believe in Jesus?

Islam was built off of Christianity, and Muslims believe Jesus to be a prophet. Christianity is built off of Judaism, and Christians believe Moses to be a prophet. What about Judaism? Do Jews believe in Jesus? Well, let's be Jewish about this: What do you mean by Jesus? If you mean Jesus as in son of God, then that's a hard no. Jews believe God is not a person, place, or thing, but rather a larger than human comprehension. The Bible speaks in metaphors, but God does not have a nose, mouth, or . . . you get the point. How about Jesus, the teacher, the student? Absolutely. The Talmud has countless examples of Jesus, referring to him as a Torah teacher,[30] referring to him as the son of Mary,[31] referring to him even as a sorcerer with disciples.[32] The Talmud also refers to him as a frivolous disciple who practices magic and turned to idolatry.[33] The Talmud even mentions Jesus's execution.[34] That's a whole lot of ink for a guy who may never have been!

JEW, SAY WHA?

"He was born, lived, and died as a Jew. Jesus's identity cannot be understood apart from his Jewishness."

Harold W. Attridge,
Professor of New Testament, Yale Divinity School

Well, that's because the rabbis differentiated between the legendary Jesus (son of God) and the historical Jesus. The historical Jesus was probably like a Reform Rabbi who called out corruption wherever he saw it.

FUN FACT!

Messianic Jews, or Jews for Jesus, believe that Jesus was the son of God and practice like "normative" Jews (lighting Shabbat candles). The thing is, every other Jewish denomination on the planet—from the most liberal to conservative—will say believing in Jesus as God's son is way out of bounds with Jewish theology.

HOW JEWISH ARE YOU?

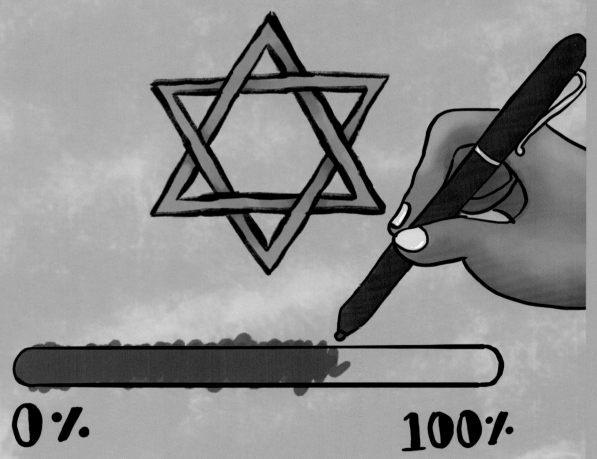

0%   100%

How Do I Know If I'm a Jew? Can I Convert?

Welcome! The Hebrew term for convert, foreigner, refugee, and stranger is *ger*, poetically connected in Hebrew to the same root word, as *gar*, which is to dwell. The Jews are told thirty-six times in the Torah not to oppress the ger and/or to love the ger, reminding the reader that "You too were *gerim* in the land of Egypt." The rabbis of the *midrash* asked, "Why was Abram known as Abram the *Ivri*, the wanderer?" Their response: "for the whole world was on one side—*meyever*—and Abram was on another,"[35] again linking "other-sider"-ness as a type of belonging DNA of the Jew. According to the sages elsewhere, anyone who exhibits loving kindness upon their fellow is certainly a descendant of Abraham, Isaac, and Jacob. And anyone who is nasty upon their fellow, well, you've got enough data to question their lineage.[36] The sages even say anyone who despises idol worship is called a Jew.[37]

Jew, say wha?

> **"**The Sages taught: With regard to a potential convert who comes to a court in order to convert, at the present time, the judges of the court say to him: What did you see that motivated you to come to convert? Don't you know that the Jewish people at the present time are anguished, suppressed, despised, and harassed, and hardships are frequently visited upon them? If he says: I know, and although I am unworthy of joining the Jewish people and sharing in their sorrow, I nevertheless desire to do so, then the court accepts him immediately to begin the conversion process. **"**
>
> *Babylonian Talmud, Yevamot 47a*

For the rabbis, Jewish identity was intertwined with how one lived in the world and whether or not one did so in a God-fearing, people-loving manner. Nowadays, we have different denominational entry points into Judaism, which include their own courses of study and pathways. Unfortunately, because conversion in Judaism is as politicized as it is, entry into one denomination does not guarantee entry into another. That's due to many reasons: differences in Jewish law, lifestyle, and plain old infighting. That being said, the myth of turning away a Jew thrice is just that—a myth. The elder sage of the Talmud Hillel would convert interested converts on the spot, little to no questions asked, and then welcome them into a study of learning. Jews come in all shapes, colors, and sizes. Judaism is not a race or ethnicity, and to quote Rabbi Abraham Infield: "Judaism is not a religion" either. What is it then? See *Why Jews Do That*.

@JennyYoungArt

GRUB

Faby Rodriguez

Why Are Jews Obsessed with Food?

"They tried to kill us, we survived, let's eat" is actually not part of the Jewish canon. In fact, the rabbis felt quite strongly about mindless eating. Maimonides wrote that, "a person who locks the gates of his courtyard and eats and drinks with his children and his wife without feeding the poor and the embittered, is not indulging in rejoicing associated with a *mitzvah*, but rather the rejoicing of his gut." In Judaism, blessings are recited at almost every waking moment, from seeing a rainbow, hearing thunder, or after having successfully gone to the bathroom. All these things are miraculous, *nu*, so why should food be any different? There are blessings to be said before and after[38] eating all different types of food. In fact, if one bottle of wine is brought to the table and then a better bottle of wine comes out, there's even a blessing for that! Blessings are about elevating our awareness to the bounty of the moment. Food is our most primal need. So, help yourself and dig in. But, before you do: bless.

JEW, SAY WHA?

"Let's rejoice today with edibles fairest, set in choice array, with morsels rarest, fat capons, quails and fish, each upon a lordly dish. "

Traditional Friday night liturgy

SHABBAT MEAL CHAMPIONSHIPS

@JennyYoungArt

FUN FACT!

The first packaged food (the fruit from the tree of knowledge) contained false advertising about its ingredients. Initially warned, "You must not eat of it; for as soon as you eat of it, you shall die."[39] Eventually, Adam and Eve were expelled. Little bite, big consequence.

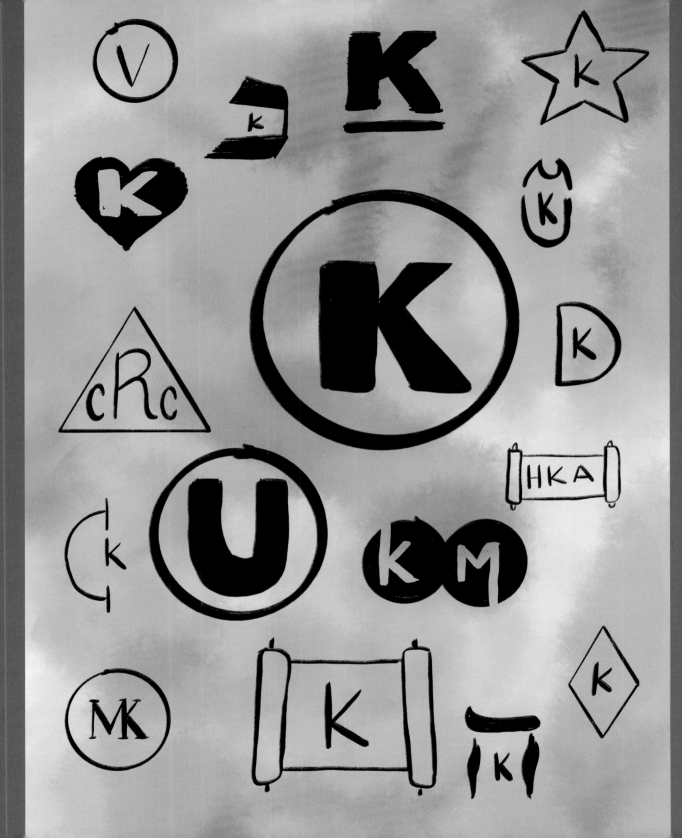

What Does Keeping Kosher Actually Mean?

Kosher literally means proper or legitimate. Keeping kosher refers to honoring and keeping the set of detailed dietary rules that govern eating. It means certain foods cannot be eaten (pork, shellfish, etc.) and it means certain foods must be separated (milk and meat, chicken and milk). It means certain foods need to be slaughtered a certain way (chicken, meat). And it means checking for a certification of aforementioned items when shopping at a supermarket. Observant Jews wait to eat dairy at least three hours after having eaten meat. This is just a short list of an encyclopedic array of laws pertaining to eating. Contrary to popular belief, it does not mean food needs to be blessed by a rabbi. Kosher meat entails a particular type of ritual slaughter, as well as an intense period of blood removal and salting. There has been a growing movement among certain religious communities to keep "ethical kashrut," with a specialized focus on treatment of animals and workers, ensuring that the food we enjoy was prepared in the most humane and ethical of circumstances.

JEW, SAY WHA?

"One who eats slowly lives long."

Babylonian Talmud, Brachot 54b

START→ →KOSHER

@JennyYoungArt

FUN FACT!

Kosher meat is considered halal. However, halal meat is not certified kosher.[40]

Ashkenazi vs. Sephardi, Slytherin vs. Gryffindor; Who Has the Better Food?

Like the Montagues and the Capulets, or the Jets and the Sharks, Judaism has plenty of their own turf wars, and none more vibrant than when it comes to cultural foods. Jews from Germany and other countries in Eastern Europe are known as Ashkenazi. Jews from areas around the Mediterranean Sea, including Portugal, Spain, the Middle East, and Northern Africa are known as Sephardic. Each community comes with its customs, traditions, and of course recipes. Bagels, babkas, borscht, and blintzes? Ashkenazi. Baba ghanoush, baklava, and bourekas? Sephardic. Knish, kugel, kreplach, and knaidlach? Ashkenazi. Couscous and falafel? Sephardic. Let your palate and stomach decide which tastes best. Either way, the blessings recited over and after food are the same.

Jew, Say Wha?

> **"**Care for your physical body in order to give the body a share of the spiritual light attained by the soul.**"**
>
> *Rebbe Nachman of Bratzlov, Likutey Moharan I, 22*

@JennyYoungArt

FUN FACT!

Cholent in Yiddish, or *Hamin* in Hebrew, is the most epic Jewish stew, and can be found in both Sephardic and Ashkenazi kitchens. Simmered for at least twelve hours and eaten traditionally on Saturday, the food cooks on Friday before the Sabbath sun sets and is kept on a hot plate throughout the day, thereby keeping with the laws that prohibit cooking on the Sabbath. Lentils, potatoes, beans, meat—the works! We've even included the recipe on page 98!

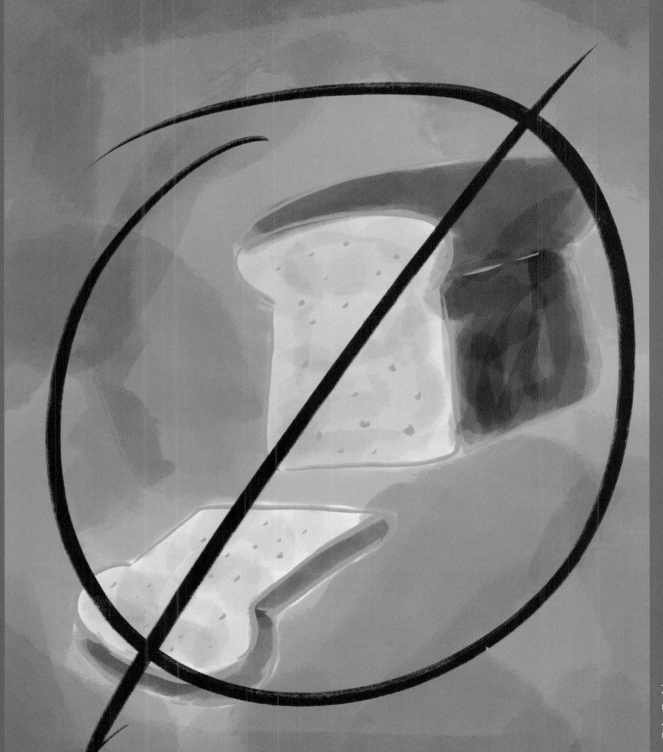

What's Kosher for Passover Food and Why Does My Grocery Store Sell It All Year?

The Bible says, "At night you shall eat matzot."[41] No, not *all* other nights. Why this one? For on this night, Passover, the springtime festival of freedom, Jews celebrate the ancient Israelites' exodus from Egypt and liberty from slavery. The saltine-like cracker, matza, is the most commonly associated Passover food; but, in truth, the category is far more expansive. There are the symbolic Passover foods like wine (four cups, drink up!), a shank bone, hard-boiled egg, bitter herb, a non-bitter vegetable, and haroset (the mortar-like fruit mixture). But there's also the food that the Torah prohibits: namely *hametz*, which refers to any leavened product (specifically, anything that rises longer than 18 minutes). So, pasta, bagels, cereal—all that's out. There is some terrible-tasting cereal that is kosher for Passover, but that's not quite in the spirit of avoiding hametz. As to why your grocer sells it year-round? Perhaps they are familiar with the teaching of Rebbe Nachman of Bratzlav who believed that "the Exodus from Egypt happens in every human being, in every era, in every year, and in every day." *Kitniyot* is a Hebrew term referring to legumes. Sefardim eat these on Passover; Ashkenazim don't, though the Conservative movement recently allowed eating these. Quinoa is also kosher for Passover.

JEW, SAY WHA?

> **"**We used to be slaves in Egypt. Now we're slaves in the kitchen.**"**
>
> *My grandma,*
> *Miriam Wolkenfeld-Cohen,*
> *Holocaust Refugee*

PASSOVER SEDER TABLE:

MOM   DAD   GUY WHO ALWAYS BRINGS UP ISRAEL

@JennyYoungArt

FUN FACT!

Though Jews are required to be rid of all hametz products over the course of Passover, if getting rid of all one's hametz causes an excessive financial burden or waste, the rabbis of yore allowed a legal loophole for Jews to sell their hametz to their non-Jewish neighbors. This is a practice that is still upheld today, meaning if you sell your scotch and cereal to Tim McDonald next door, technically, he can come over during the week and take a drink, no questions asked, because it's no longer yours.

How Kosher Is Sex?

The first commandment in the Torah is understood to be "be fruitful and multiply"[42] (i.e., get it on!). While this is generally understood to be in the context of a heteronormative marriage, the times they are a changin'. Reform, Conservative, and Reconstructionist Jews perform marriage ceremonies for LGBTQ Jews; the Orthodox community is predominantly opposed, though this too is evolving. "It is not good for a human to be alone,"[43] God says in Genesis, and one needn't look past *Song of Songs* for erotic Biblical literature (though the rabbis felt strongly that this text was a metaphorical allegory between God and the people of Israel. Sure.). Marriage is still sacred in Judaism and reserves its role as the primary playground for all sexual play. In a committed relationship, Jewish law's view on sex is pretty permissive, though it often gets painted in puritanical strokes (see the *Curb Your Enthusiasm* hole in sheet farce). Once consent has been affirmed, Maimonides believes it's all kosher in the bedroom.[44] Just have your safe words ready. According to Jewish law, men and women ought not to engage in sex during a woman's menstrual cycle, and a woman must go to the mikvah (ritual bath) for immersion in order to resume relations.

JEW, SAY WHA?

> "A man is forbidden to compel his wife to have marital relations. . . . Rabbi Joshua ben Levi similarly stated: Whoever compels his wife to have marital relations will have unworthy children. . . . Rabbi Yochanan observed: If the Torah had not been given, we could have learned modesty from the cat, honesty from the ant, chastity from the dove, and good manners from the rooster, who first coaxes and then mates."
>
> *Babylonian Talmud, Eruvin 100b*

Since having sex is considered a mitzvah and having Sabbath pleasure (a.k.a., *oneg Shabbat*) is also a mitzvah, many an adolescent religious teen have referenced the importance of the "double mitzvah" (i.e., Shabbos sex).

@JennyYoungArt

FUN FACT!

Just like other populations—though perhaps heightened because of such conservative practices governing sexual relations—there is a prevalence of sex- and pornography-related addictions and rehabilation treatments in the Orthodox community.

Faby Rodriguez

Is Pot Kosher?

The Bible refers to the ancient sacrifices as having "pleasant fragrance to the Divine."[45] Now, extending that to reefer's reek may be a bit of a stretch, but a snuff box (usually tobacco) was indeed passed around in synagogue before Torah service to make sure folks were awake (and is still done so in certain Orthodox communities). Marijuana is not explicitly mentioned in the Torah, but Rabbi Moshe Feinstein, a prominent rabbi of the past century, did prohibit its use in a responsum of his. In it, he writes that it physically injures, though critics have responded that, if so, alcohol and cigarettes should also be deemed as *treyf* (off limits). Now, as medical marijuana becomes increasingly popular and recreational marijuana is legally permitted in certain states, edible marijuana products do in fact have kosher certifications.

JEW, SAY WHA?

"The most serious challenges to Judaism posed by modern thought and experience are, to me, game theory and psychedelic experience. Once I realize the game structure of my commitments, once I see how all my theologizing is just an elaborate death struggle between my soul and the God within her, or when I can undergo the deepest cosmic experience via some miniscule quantity of organic alkaloids or LSD, then the whole validity of my ontological assertions is in doubt. But game theory works the other way too. God is playing a game of hide-and-seek with himself and me. The psychedelic experience can be not only a challenge but also a support of my faith. After seeing what really happens at the point where all is one and where God-immanent surprises God-transcendent and they merge in cosmic laughter, I can also see Judaism in a new and amazing light. "

Rabbi Zalman Schachter-Shalomi,

founder of Renewal Judaism

@JennyYoungArt

FUN FACT!

Marijuana is a plant and so kosher certification is not required for the plant itself.
Some religious Jews even recite a blessing before inhaling.[46]

GOD

Muslims Pray Five Times a Day; What about Jews?

If you have ever flown to Israel on El-Al Airlines (that's Israel's national airline), you may have noticed a group of Orthodox men congregating at the back of the plane, inadvertently blocking the bathrooms. They aren't necessarily trying to be rude; they're trying to fulfill a commandment to pray three times a day: evening, morning, and afternoon. (When does the sun rise on a trip to Australia? Check with your local rabbi.) Rabbinic legend is that each of the patriarchs instituted a different prayer service.[47] Other rabbis believe the prayers to be in lieu of the sacrifices which were once offered daily at the ancient Temple in Jerusalem. There are special prayers added on the Sabbath: On Friday night there is *Kabbalat Shabbat*, the service which welcomes in the Sabbath. On Saturday and holidays, there's *Musaf*, literally meaning the additional service. Besides sacred days, there are blessings that can be recited on any day of the week: from waking up in the morning, to donning new clothing, to seeing a sage of great renown, and even upon seeing a friend you haven't seen in a year.[48]

JEW, SAY WHA?

"I felt my legs were praying."

Rabbi Abraham Joshua Heschel
after marching in Selma
with his friend, the Reverend Dr.
Martin Luther King Jr.

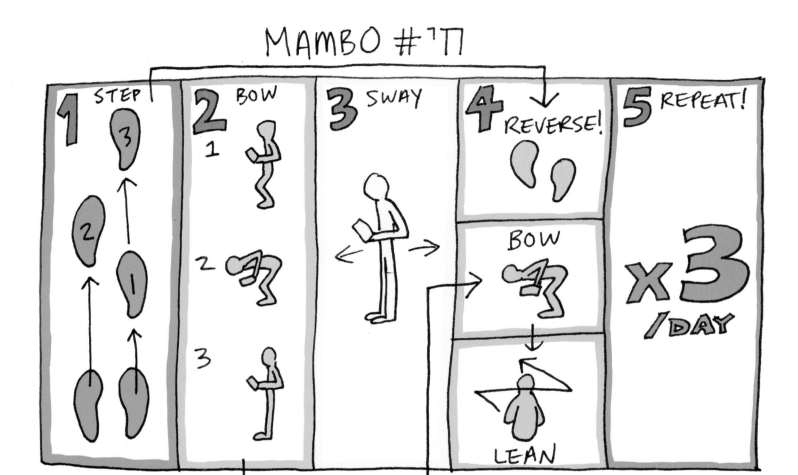

FUN FACT!

Rabbi Samson Raphael Hirsch, a German Orthodox rabbi of the 1800s, noted that the Hebrew word meaning prayer, *hitpalel*, is the reflexive form of a verb meaning "to judge." He wrote that prayer, therefore, "denotes judging oneself, or coming to a correct opinion of oneself, or at last, an inner attempt to accomplish this."

How Do Jews Pray?

Put your left foot in, put your right foot out. Just kidding, though there is a bunch of choreography that is involved in Jewish prayer: beating of the chest, kneeling, bowing, *shuckling*. Jews read prayers that have been recited for thousands of years and Jews recite prayers daily. We sing, dance, cry, laugh—all are forms of prayer. The Talmud discussed at length whether prayer should be fixed or free,[49] as in, mass starts at seven, or whenever the spirit moves you. Both polarities are inherently part of Judaism. The mystics valued informal, impromptu prayer tremendously, traveling to the forests to be about nature and practice silent screaming, singing, dancing, or just speaking openly to the Divine. Jews sway, eyes closed, yearning, seeking, begging, pleading, demanding. The founder of Jewish mysticism, the Baal Shem Tov, believed that prayer was union with the *Shechina*, the feminine name for the Divine Presence. And so, just as two people might move their bodies back and forth as they begin lovemaking, so too ought a person sway their body in a rhythmic fashion while praying. Dig it.

Jew, Say Wha?

> **"**Prayer is meaningless unless it is subversive, unless it seeks to overthrow and to ruin the pyramids of callousness, hatred, opportunism, and falsehood. The liturgical movement must become a revolutionary movement, seeking to overthrow the forces that continue to destroy the promise, the hope, the vision.**"**
>
> *Rabbi Abraham Joshua Heschel*

JEWISH PRAYER MOVES

@JennyYoungArt

FUN FACT!

The *shmoneh esreh*, also known as the silent meditation or the *Amidah*, is prayed thrice daily and must be recited standing, with one's feet touching for the duration of the prayer. That being said, the tale is told of the Talmudic Rabbi Akiva who, once left alone to pray the silent devotional prayer, would start in one part of the room and end in another.[50]

Faby Rodriguez

Do Jews Go to Confession Like Catholics?

"Forgive me, Father, for I have sinned." Believe it or not that phrase exists in Hebrew liturgy as well. *Slach na, avinu, ki chatanu.* The difference? In Judaism it's all in plural. *Forgive us, our Father, for we have sinned.* Jews do not confess to people, but rather confess their sins to God directly. Hence, the beating of the chest on Yom Kippur, the portion in the weekly prayers which asks God for forgiveness. Note: Sins between God and humans, God can forgive, but sins between humans and humans God cannot forgive.[51] There is a special confession, *vidui* in Hebrew, recited on one's deathbed as well.

Jew, say wha?

> "*Ashamnu*—we have trespassed; *Bagadnu*—we have dealt treacherously; *Gazalnu*—we have robbed; *Dibarnu dofi*—we have spoken slander; *He'evinu*—we have acted perversely; *V'hirshanu*—we have done wrong; *Zadnu*—we have acted presumptuously; *Hamasnu*—we have done violence; *Tafalnu sheker*—we have practiced deceit; *Yaatsnu ra*—we have counseled evil *Kizavnu*—we have spoken falsehood; *Latsnu*—we have scoffed; *Maradnu*—we have revolted; *Niatsnu*—we have blasphemed; *Sararnu*—we have rebelled; *Avinu*—we have committed iniquity; *Pashanu*—we have transgressed; *Tsararnu*—we have oppressed; *Kishinu oref*—we have been stiff-necked; *Rashanu*—we have acted wickedly; *Shichatnu*—we have dealt corruptly; *Tiavnu*—we have committed abomination; *Tainu*—we have gone astray; *Titanu*—we have led others astray."
>
> *Yom Kippur Liturgy*

@JennyYoungArt

FUN FACT!

In the times of the Temple, on Yom Kippur, the Jewish Day of Atonement, the high priest would "cast" the sins of Israel onto a goat, thereby, literally creating the concept of a scapegoat.

Who, What, Where, When, How, and Why God?

Elie Wiesel remembers witnessing three men put God on trial at Auschwitz. After the trial finished (where the court found God guilty), the men say, "Come, time to *daven maariv*." Or, "It's time to pray the evening service." If anyone tries to tell you why bad things happen to good people, they're trying to sell you something and you should run as fast as possible. God in the Five Books of Moses can be angry, vengeful, passionate. God in the Prophets is compassionate, loving, forgiving, and jealous. God in the Writings is more absent as humans become more and more of the protagonists (which was always God's intention).[52] God is what God will be, says God to Moses when they first "meet." God wants the heart, say the mystics . . . as in, no bullcrap. The Bible, which traditionalists attribute to God, affirms that every person is created in the image of the Divine, but also precludes priests with blemishes from serving in the Temple. That same book says men who have sex with each other should be stoned, and to love your neighbor as yourself. It's almost as if the Bible anticipated Walt Whitman's response, "Do I contradict myself? Very well, then I contradict myself. I am large. I contain multitudes."[53]

JEW, SAY WHA?

> **"**Rav Zutra bar Tovia said that Rav said, God says: May it be My Will that My mercy will overcome My anger, and may my compassion prevail over my other attributes, may I conduct towards my children with love, and may I enter before them beyond the letter of the law. **》》**
>
> *Babylonian Talmud, Berachot 7a*

FUN FACT!

God's first question, as recorded in the Bible, is: "Where are you?"[54] This is a question Jewish mystics believe applies to every person who reads the question.

I WANT TO BELIEVE

Faby Rodriguez

What If I Don't Believe Any of This Crap?

Welcome to the tribe! Let's remember: Judaism spans thousands of years of history. The ancients didn't have too many atheists in their flock. Then again, belief didn't become a codified part of Judaism until Maimonides came along in the Middle Ages. In Judaism, the notion of commandments (i.e., responsibility) is central. God gives commandments that are horizontal and vertical, or commandments which govern human behavior toward fellow human beings (not oppressing the stranger, giving tzedaka), and between humans and the Divine (Sabbath, dietary laws). The rabbis said giving tzedaka is equal in importance to all other commandments combined.[55] The implication seems to be: What you do matters more than what you believe. As the Torah says, "Do what is right and good (in the sight of God)."[56] You got this.

JEW, SAY WHA?

> **"**1. I believe in the existence of the Creator, who is perfect in every manner of existence and is the Primary Cause of all that exists. 2. I believe in God's absolute and unparalleled unity. 3. I believe in God's non-corporeality, nor that He will be affected by any physical occurrences, such as movement, or rest, or dwelling. 4. I believe in God's eternity. 5. I believe in the imperative to worship God exclusively and no foreign false gods. 6. I believe that God communicates with man through prophecy. 7. I believe in the primacy of the prophecy of Moses our teacher. 8. I believe in the divine origin of the Torah. 9. I believe in the immutability of the Torah. 10. I believe in God's omniscience and providence. 11. I believe in divine reward and retribution. 12. I believe in the arrival of the Messiah and the messianic era. 13. I believe in the resurrection of the dead.**"**
>
> *Maimonides's 13 Principles of Faith*

@JennyYoungArt

FUN FACT!

The rabbis believed that all of Israel is under the assumption of keeping kosher
(until you know one may not). That is to say that all Jews are *believed* to be God-fearing,
observant, and righteous until you know otherwise.

Acknowledgments

"We begin with acknowledging the hosts," say the sages of the Talmud. Thanks to the Host of Hosts, the Creator of All, Jah Bless, for giving me life and bringing me to this moment in time.

This book would simply not be if it were not for the sage counsel and advice of Marshall Sonenshine, a mentsh par excellence, who has supported me since the sukkah and beyond. Thanks for your patience and persistence with this project.

To Tony and Matt, Karen, and the whole team at Skyhorse Publishing for birthing this book into reality, thanks for taking a risk on a young renegade, vagabond rabbi.

To the Base chevreh: the fam of students and fellow soul teachers who remind me why I do what I do.

To Jenny and Faby, the most talented artists and big-hearted collaborators. Your images made these words come alive.

To Hanan David of Queens and Long Iowa Island, thank you for the reminder to laugh amid the darkness.

To Shira, steak's on me; thank you for supporting my schemes in all your ways.

To Chloe, Avi, Mike, and the HMI family, for expanding my heart and horizons by the Sea of Galilee.

To Hillel, OOI fam, and the ChInO, who has believed in me since kiddush—thank you.

To all those who gave this a peek and didn't dissuade me from pursuing: Elisha, Braude, Suzanne, Potek.

Thank you to my English teacher in 9th grade, who gave me a D- on my first high school paper, and to my 5th grade Mishna teacher who, after seeing me doodle Hasidic rabbis and scandalously dressed ladies in my textbook, didn't scold me but instead gently asked me to devote my drawing elsewhere.

To all my family members who believed in me more than I do myself: Tati, Ma, Moish, Miss, Sar, Bubz.

To my forever editor, Yaeli, who holds my heart's keys.

For all the teachers out there who aren't afraid of a question, you never know which snarky student may end up a rabbi.

What Jew Say? Phrases, Places, Names, Terms, and Ideas

Aleychem Shalom
Unto you peace
(reply to Shalom Aleychem).

Avraham, Yitzchak, Yakov
The Biblical patriarchs: Abraham, Isaac and Jacob.

Beit HaMikdash
Refers to the ancient temple(s) in Jerusalem. Literally: house of holiness.

Beit Kneset
Synagogue. Literally: house of gathering.

Beit Midrash
A study hall. Literally: house of seeking.

Bentch
Yiddish for bless.
Typically refers to the grace after meals.

Bikur Cholim
Visiting the sick, a commandment.

Chag sameach
Happy holiday in Hebrew.

Chillul Hashem
A desecration of the Divine name.

Daven
Yiddish for "to pray."

Derekh Eretz
Common courtesy. Literally: the way of the land.

Eyzer Knegdo
Helpmate, life partner.

Gut Shabbes
Literally, a good Sabbath.
A typical Sabbath greeting in Yiddish.

Gut vokh
Literally, a good week. A typical greeting post-Sabbath in Yiddish.

Gut yomtev, gut yor
Literally, a good holiday, a good year. A typical holiday greeting in Yiddish.

Halacha
Jewish law. The Hebrew shoresh, root word of halacha, though, is halach, which connotes going or being on a journey. Jewish pathways.

Hachnasat Orchim
The mitzvah of welcoming guests.

Kashrut
Dietary laws.

Kiddush Hashem
A sanctification of the Divine name.

Lashon Hara
Literally, wicked speech, evil tongue, also known as gossip or slander.

Machloket l'shem Shamayim
Arguments for the sake of Heaven.

Middah
A characteristic or trait.

Mitzvah
A commandment.

Refuah Sheleimah
A complete healing.

Sarah, Rivka, Rachel, Leah
The Biblical matriarchs.

Shabbat Shalom
A peaceful Sabbath. A typical Sabbath greeting in Hebrew.

Shalom
Peace, goodbye, hello, a name of God, and related to the idea of wholeness.

Shalom Aleychem
Peace unto you (a greeting), also a song sung at Shabbat dinners, also a famous Yiddish writer.

Shalom Bayit
Maintaining peace in the home.

Shanda Far Di Goyim
A shameful embarrassment before the gentiles.

Shavua tov
Literally, a good week. A typical greeting post-Sabbath in Hebrew.

Tefilah
Prayer.

Teshuva
Return, forgiveness. According to the rabbis of the Talmud[57], teshuva is so dank it hastens redemption and transforms intentional sins into meritorious deeds.

Tikun Olam
Repairing the world.

Torah
The Bible, learning, soul teaching.

Tzelem Elokim
[The belief that every individual is created in] God's divine image.

Yetzer Tov/Ra
The good/evil inclination every human being possesses.

---

[57]Babylonian Talmud, Tractate Yoma 86b

Endnotes

[1] Genesis 4:9

[2] 39 Creative Labors: Planting, plowing, reaping, gathering, threshing, winnowing, sorting, dissecting, sifting, kneading, cooking, shearing, laundering, carding wool, dyeing, spinning, kneading, warping, threading, weaving, separating, tying, untying, sewing, tearing, trapping, killing, skinning, preserving, smoothing, scoring, cutting, writing, erasing, constructing, deconstructing, extinguishing fire, igniting fire, fine tuning, transferring between domains, etc.

[3] Babylonian Talmud Pesachim 106a, "The verse reads: 'Remember the Sabbath and keep it holy.' This means, 'Remember the Sabbath over a cup of wine at the onset of the Sabbath.'"

[4] Maimonides Laws of Shabbat 5:1

[5] Also known as Shalom *bayit*, literally meaning, peace in the home.

[6] *Pikauch Nefesh*—saving a soul.

[7] Except for three: Babylonian Talmud Sanhedrin 74a teaches one can't commit murder, perform licentious sexual acts, or worship idols to save one's life.

[8] Proverbs 20:25 "God's candle is a human soul."

[9] Rabbi Yosef Karo Shulkhan Arukh 694

[10] Rabbi Moshe Isserlis Shulchan Arukh 696:8

[11] Rabbi Yosef Karo Shulchan Arukh 695:2

[12] While there are *shiurim*/measured portions of water that scholars of Jewish law dictate may be consumed for people who are sick or pregnant women, most Orthodox rabbis today find such a practice harmful, wrong, and therefore unnecessary for people who suffer from eating disorders.

[13] Rabbi Yosef Karo Orach Chayim, Laws of Fasting, 580:3

[14] Magen Avraham; Rabbi Avraham Gombiner on Laws of Hanukkah.

[15] http://www.pewresearch.org/fact-tank/2014/04/14/attending-a-seder-is-common-practice-for-american-jews/

[16] Rabbi Ya'akov taught: "This world is compared to an ante-chamber that leads to OlamHa–Ba, (the World-to-Come)" (PirkeiAvot4:21).

[17] Deuteronomy 30:19: "I call heaven and earth to witness against you this day: I have put before you life and death, blessing and curse. Choose life."

[18] Babylonian Talmud, Kiddushin 31a.

[19] http://www.pewresearch.org/fact-tank/2016/04/20/what-different-styles-of-head-coverings-say-about-israeli-jewish-men/

[20] http://www.yivoencyclopedia.org/article.aspx/Dress

[21] Deuteronomy 6:8

[22] Numbers 15:37-39: "The Lord said to Moses as follows: Speak to the Israelite people and instruct them to make for themselves fringes on the corners of their garments throughout the ages; let them attach a cord of blue to the fringe at each corner. That shall be your fringe; look at it and recall all the commandments of the Lord and observe them, so that you do not follow your heart and eyes in your lustful urge."

[23] Shulchan Aruch 23:1

[24] Rabbi Yosef Karo, Shulkhan Arukh, Orach Chayim 271:4; 299:1

[25] Not immersing dishes in the mikvah does not make the food unkosher.

[26] Exodus 32:9

[27] Deuteronomy 11, 13-21: "Take care not to be lured away to serve other gods and bow to them. For the LORD's anger will flare up against you, and He will shut up the skies so that there will be no rain and the ground will not yield its produce; and you will soon perish from the good land that the LORD is assigning to you."

[28] Genesis 32:29

[29] As in "Tzedek, tzedek—Justice, justice, shall you pursue," Deuteronomy 16:20

[30] Babylonian Talmud Avoda Zara 17a, Hulin 2:24

[31] Babylonian Talmud Shabbat 104b, Sanhedrin 67a

[32] Babylonian Talmud Sanhedrin 43ab

[33] Babylonian Talmud Sotah 47a, Sanhedrin 107b

[34] Babylonian Talmud Sanhedrin 43-ab

[35] Bresheet Rabbah 42:8

[36] Midrash Lekakh Tov Genesis 50 Vayechi.

[37] Babylonian Talmud Megilah 13

38 Birkat HaMazon, the grace after meals, is recited after partaking in a meal that includes bread. The Bracha Achrona, the after blessing, is recited after eating other food products.

39 Genesis 2

40 https://muslimmatters.org/2012/06/22/is-kosher-meat-%E1%B8%A5alal-a-comparison-of-the-halakhic-and-shar%CA%BFi-requirements-for-animal-slaughter/

41 Exodus 12:18

42 Genesis 1:28

43 Genesis 2:18

44 Rambam Hilchot Issurei Biah 21:9 "A man's own wife is permitted to him [once consent has been confirmed], and therefore whatever a man wants to do with his wife he may do. He can have sex with her whenever he pleases, kiss any part of her body that he wants, and have sex with her in the normal way and in the non-normal way, or sex by 'way of her limbs' [i.e. oral sex]."

45 Leviticus 1:9

46 Rabbi Chaim Kanievsky, a leading Ultra-Orthodox scholar of Jewish law, had the blessing over spices recited: "Blessed are you, Adonai, our God, creator of varied types of spices."

The *Englewooder Rebbetzin* Tali Pniefsky's Epic Cholent Recipe

1 package cholent beans mix

1 package barley

1/2 bag farro

3 cubed sweet potatoes

2 cubed Yukon gold potatoes

2 large pieces flanken meat

1/2 packet onion soup mix

Long squeeze of ketchup (approximately 10 seconds)

Medium-ish squeeze of hot sauce (your choice!)

A lot of paprika

A few shakes of Lawry's seasoned salt

Put all items in crockpot and cook on high for 20 minutes, then switch temperature to low and cook for an additional 20 hours.

[47] Babylonian Talmud, Brachot 26b

[48] "Blessed are you God, our God, Sovereign of the Universe, who has fashioned the human being with wisdom and created within them many openings and holes; it is revealed and known before you that if one of them were to be opened or ruptured it would be impossible to stand before your throne of glory for even an hour. Blessed are you, God, who heals flesh and acts wondrously." —Traditional liturgy, blessing recited after using the bathroom.

[49] "Rabbi Elazar said: Always let a man test himself: if he can direct his heart, let him pray; if he cannot, let him not pray." —Babylonian Talmud, Berachot 30b

[50] "When he was with the congregation, he would pray quickly so as not to be a burden on those praying with him [who would respectfully wait for him to finish]. But when he prayed alone, one could leave him in one corner and afterwards find him in another corner, due to his many bows and prostrations." —Babylonian Talmud, Berachot 31a

[51] Mishna Yoma Chapter 8:9: "For transgressions between human and God Yom Kippur effects atonement, but for transgressions between human and fellow Yom Kippur does not effect atonement, until one has pacified one's fellow."

[52] Genesis 9:2: "Everything with which the earth is astir - and upon all the fish of the sea; they are given into your hand."

[53] "Song of Myself" by Walt Whitman.

[54] Genesis 3:9

[55] Babylonian Talmud, Bava Batra 9a

[56] Deuteronomy 6:18

About the Author

AVRAM MLOTEK is a rabbi, cantor, actor, and writer. A grandchild of Holocaust refugees and Yiddish cultural icons, he has been named as one of "America's Most Inspiring Rabbis" by *The Forward* (and that was before he co-officiated a wedding with the Notorious RBG (Justice Ruth Bader Ginsburg)). He is a founder of Base, an international home-centered ministry which works with millennial Jews worldwide, where he serves as Director of Spiritual Life. Instagram: @avrammlotek; Twitter: @RabbiAvMlotek

FABY RODRIGUEZ is a graphic designer from Mexico. She has focused her career in print media working in newspapers for both Mexico and more than ten states in the US. Follow her on Instagram at @favsdoodles.

JENNY YOUNG is an artist based in Philadelphia. She likes to draw dark and satirical cartoons commenting on modern politics, technology, and spirituality. Follow her on Instagram at @jennyyoungart.